Glory in His Name

A Daily Devotional on the Names and Titles of God

DR. WIL CHEVALIER

WESTBOW
PRESS®
A DIVISION OF THOMAS NELSON
& ZONDERVAN

WestBow Press books may be ordered through booksellers or by contacting:

WestBow Press
A Division of Thomas Nelson & Zondervan
1663 Liberty Drive
Bloomington, IN 47403
www.westbowpress.com
1 (866) 928-1240

Scripture quotations marked NASB are taken from the New American Standard Bible, Copyright 1960, 1962, 1963, 1968, 1971, 1972, 1973, 1975, 1977, 1995 by The Lockman Foundation. Used by permission.

ISBN: 978-1-5127-7379-8 (sc)
ISBN: 978-1-5127-7380-4 (hc)
ISBN: 978-1-5127-7378-1 (e)

Library of Congress Control Number: 2017901761

Print information available on the last page.

WestBow Press rev. date: 4/28/2017

Contents

Acknowledgments

Special thanks and my deepest gratitude to: Alyssa Carr, Dr. Maynard Eyestone, Rev. James Folkers, Jeanette Morris, and Susan Titus-Osborne for their outstanding editorial assistance.

In addition, I would like to acknowledge the insightful input on the original manuscript from: Drs. Luis Pantoja, James C. De Young, Ron Brewer, and Professors David Solstrom, Larry Waters, and James R. Whelchel.

Foreword

As his pastor for many years, I can attest that Dr. Wil Chevalier knows God through developing a deep faith in Christ, which led to a dramatic change in his life. He loves Scripture, having memorized large portions of it. His theological education and remarkable missionary ministry for over 35 years has led to the mentoring and discipling of hundreds, and they have in turn carried on similar ministries that have spread to several nations. I know of no other discipling ministry as fruitful as his.

A.W. Tozer says in his book, *The Knowledge of the Holy,* that "the mightiest thought the mind can entertain is the thought of God, and the weightiest word in any language is its word for God." Scripture, the source for knowing God, His character, and His works, gives many names for God. Dr. Chevalier's book, *Glory in His Name,* contains thirty-one meditations about the wonderful God whom Christians worship via many of His scriptural names.

The apostle Paul prays for Christians that they would be "filled with the knowledge of His will in all spiritual wisdom and understanding so that they may walk in a manner worthy of the Lord, to please Him in all respects, bearing fruit in every good work and increasing in the knowledge of God" (Col. 1:9, 10). This same "knowledge of God," leading to transformed living, will be yours through a thoughtful reading of Dr. Chevalier's book, *Glory in His Name.*

Pastor Jim Folkers

Although the dimensions of God's character transcend human exploration and comprehension, the biblical names of God expounded in this well-researched book by Dr. Chevalier is an awesome unveiling of His majesty. The person desiring a greater understanding of who God is and longing for a more intimate relationship with Him must read *Glory in His Name.*

Dr. H. Jack Morris
Founding Pastor
Largo Community Church

Introduction

Our body needs nourishment to be healthy, and so does our soul. The Word of God provides this nourishment for our spiritual health and growth as followers of Jesus Christ. Yet, comparatively few who occasionally read the Bible are aware of the awe-inspiring and worship-provoking majesty of the names and titles of God. I invite you to take time to read the Scripture passages for each day before reading the devotional thoughts.

This devotional guide is provided to help us meditate more fully on His greatness from a theological perspective. Jesus is the manifestation of God the Father. The greatness of Christ explains the greatness of the Father. "God is Spirit" (John 4:24), and can only be known spiritually. But fallen man is not spiritually attuned to God. Unless he is born again, he cannot see the things of God (John 3:3), much less comprehend them (1 Cor. 2:14). We become one of God's own by "believing in His name," which means believing that Jesus as the eternal Creator became one of us, took our sin upon Himself, died on the cross, rose from the dead, and is again with God the Father, interceding for us.

These varying names are but a small reflection of God's total being. The Bible also presents the nature of God in several different titles, which more informally express various facets of His character. He is so majestic and glorious that neither one nor the totality of all names or titles can adequately express His fullness. Although God reveals Himself through His names, we can still only know Him "in part." "For now we see in a mirror dimly, but then face to face" (1 Cor. 13:12). His names speak of His nature, and in order to comprehend them, even in part, we must be partakers of that nature.

No outline of the names and titles of God can present a total picture, for "His greatness is unsearchable" (Psalm 145:3). Yet, the Bible makes it abundantly clear that whatever is necessary for us to know about God can be known. In these names and titles there seems to be a progressive revelation of God's meeting every need as it arises in the experience of His people. We see that He is at work, saving, sustaining, strengthening, and sanctifying, meeting the developing spiritual life and needs of His people.

The Holy Spirit illumines our hearts to reveal to us "the knowledge of the glory of God in the face of Christ" (2 Cor. 4:6). Even though that spiritual knowledge is fragmentary, the believer needs to "grow" in the grace and knowledge of the Lord Jesus (2 Pet. 3:18).

The principal aim of this book is to help us "walk in a manner worthy of the Lord, to please Him in all respects, bearing fruit in every good work and increasing in the knowledge of God" (Col. 1:10). It is designed to help us grow by meditating on God's greatness. Please begin with prayer, asking the Lord for guidance, expressing dependence on Him to obey His Word. It has been said that "prayer is the mightiest force in the universe," and most of us would agree that there is power in prayer. Yet we often spend so little time praying. Let us ask God to cause these daily meditations on His names to lead us to a dynamic discovery of His sufficiency in the midst of any situation we may face.

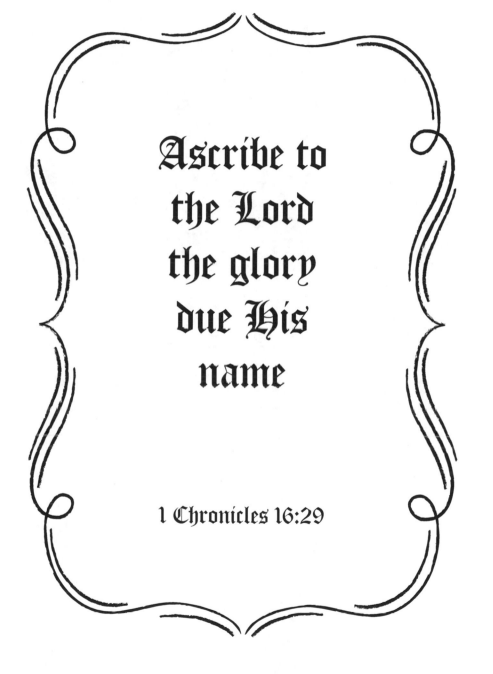

Ascribe to the Lord the glory due His name

1 Chronicles 16:29

Angel of the Lord
Anointed
Abba
Architect
Advocate
Alpha

1

The Old Testament appearances of Christ as the *Angel of the Lord*[1] have their significance in the fact that He has always sought to manifest Himself to His people.

God made known long beforehand what title His *Anointed*[2] One, the Messiah, would receive. The prophecy of Jesus' anointing is found in Psalm 45:7-8: "You have loved righteousness and hated wickedness; therefore God, Your God, has anointed You with the oil of joy above Your fellows." Jesus speaks of His anointing in Isaiah 61:1: "The Spirit of the Lord GOD is upon me, because the LORD has anointed me to bring good news to the afflicted." The anointing is for power and for understanding of God's truth.

"Abba" is an Aramaic word which speaks of a close relationship—the relationship of endearment. A slave was not allowed to address his master as "Abba." As believers, we have the privilege of calling Him *Abba! Father!*[3] and knowing that He is our provider. Knowing Him personally in such an endearing relationship can have a profound effect upon us as we continue to discover our Savior's greatness.

As the *Architect*,[4] God not only knows the end from the beginning, but He also planned, fixed, and directed everything from the beginning. While God is the Architect of the whole universe, He is also our Architect, putting things in their proper places and making something beautiful and useful of our lives.

As *Advocate*,[5] He is the Divine Lawyer who pleads our case. This name does not suggest that Jesus died to placate God's anger against sin alone and is now pleading with Him to persuade Him to forgive us. On the contrary, Jesus is our defense attorney against all of Satan's accusations. His defense? The price is already paid.

Jesus is the *Alpha*[6] and is the beginning of everything good. In Revelation 1:8 and 21:6, God is described as the Alpha and Omega. It is used in the sense that both the beginning and end, and all in between, must be related to God. This concept encompasses the whole span of history in terms of God's activity.

> *The name of the LORD is a strong tower; the righteous runs*
> *into it and is safe.* (Proverbs 18:10).

The Lord is seeking to manifest Himself to us today. We have good news to share with others: our relationship with the Father is made possible through Jesus Christ who died on the cross that we might be reconciled unto God. He wants to manifest His presence in our lives to assure us that He is able to triumph over every obstacle and opposition. He is worthy of our greatest gift, our noblest act of service, our very lives. Let us praise Him for His worthy character right now.

> *He is the Architect of my life;*
> *The Advocate pleading my case against the enemy's strife.*
> *As Abba, He is so dear to me,*
> *Almighty, what a wonderful reality.*

Read the Scriptures below and write out specific ways to put the truths from today's reading into action in your own life. Refer to the *Personal Application Diary.*

[1] Exodus 3:2; [2] Psalm 2:2; [3] Mark 14:36; [4] Hebrews 11:10; [5] 1 John 2:1; [6] Revelation 1:8.

Personal Application Diary

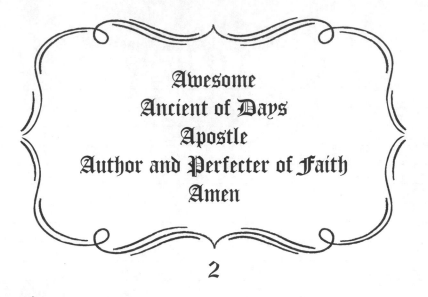

Awesome
Ancient of Days
Apostle
Author and Perfecter of Faith
Amen

2

God has been glorified by creation, providence, and redemption. As we gaze upon His beauty and become more and more aware of His redeeming love, we will want to know Him in a progressively deeper way. He is truly *Awesome*[1] and can be known only as He is revealed to the heart by the Holy Spirit.

God is revealed as the *Ancient of Days*,[2] and there never was a time that Christ did not exist, because Jesus is God. As His children, we have free access to His eternal throne of grace and to the Holy Spirit who comforts our souls. A person cannot trust human nature, but he can put full confidence in God. He is ever the same, and the permanence of His character guarantees the fulfillment of His promises: "'For the mountains may be removed and the hills may shake, but My lovingkindness will not be removed from you, and My covenant of peace will not be shaken,' says the LORD who has compassion on you" (Isaiah 54:10).

An *Apostle*[3] is one sent forth; this describes Jesus' relationship to the Father. How thankful we should be that we have salvation in Christ Jesus! We may well confess, "For from Him and through Him and to Him are all things. To Him be the glory forever. Amen" (Romans 11:36).

Faith is confidence in God that leads us to believe His Word, the Bible. And it is by faith that we receive Jesus Christ as our Lord and Savior and confess Him to the world. There can be no dealings with the Invisible God without faith in His existence. He is the origin of salvation, the *Author and Perfecter of Faith*.[4] The Bible makes it clear that faith alone cannot save us. It declares the necessity of faith in the divine person of Jesus Christ. Faith in God is putting confidence in Him and in His Word, resting on the atoning sacrifice of the Author and Perfecter of Faith. Our faithful Father has placed the final seal of His promises in the *Amen*.[5]

> *The* LORD *also will be a stronghold for the oppressed, a stronghold in times of trouble; and those who know Your name will put their trust in You* (Psalm 9:9-10).

We need faith in Christ alone to secure our eternal salvation. Our faith, however, must grow in order that we not only know Him as Savior but also as Lord. As we concentrate on growing in our reverence and awe for God and in our understanding of His love for us, we will find that our desire for Him will grow. God's Word gives us the confidence to endure trials, testings, temptations, and tribulations. Though believers may have reasons to be discouraged, we have far more reasons to rejoice.

> *The Ancient of Days from all eternity;*
> *The Awesome God has been revealed to me.*
> *The Apostle sent from above,*
> *The Amen is the seal of His love.*

Read the Scriptures below and write out specific ways to put the truths from today's reading into action in your own life. Refer to the *Personal Application Diary*.

[1] Nehemiah 1:5; [2] Daniel 7:9; [3] Hebrews 3:1; [4] Hebrews 12:2; [5] Revelation 3:14.

Personal Application Diary

Breath of the Almighty
Branch
Beloved Son
Bridegroom
Bread of Life
Beginning

3

Through the *Breath of the Almighty*,[1] the Spirit gives us life and strength. In all of life's situations, we who are His children can experience a deep, settled peace as we trust in Him. This title shows that the Spirit's action is heavenly; that which comes from above is sovereign, and is infinitely above man. The Spirit is the manifestation of God's very presence in our lives.

Jesus, who is the *Branch*[2] and of divine origin, is a descendant of David. He transcends our understanding and cannot be fully comprehended by finite intelligence. Jesus Christ is perfectly loved by God the Father and is God's own Unique One, His *Beloved Son*.[3]

Jesus is the *Bridegroom*[4] and is betrothed to the Church, His bride. As the Bridegroom, He longs to become ever more unified with His bride. Individual worshipers may not be conscious of God's presence as they meditate upon His perfections, but as they walk closely and obediently with Him they will sense His transforming power.

During the last evening with His disciples in the upper room, Jesus gave instructions for His own memorial service. He took, blessed, and broke the bread and explained its significance as He gave it to His disciples to eat. Then He took the cup and explained its meaning as He gave it to them to drink. It was not enough for the bread to be broken and the wine to be poured out. His disciples were not simply spectators. They had to eat and drink. The bread and wine entered the physical body, giving it life and health. This symbolism offers us a dramatic picture of the life of Christ entering spiritually into the life of the believer. Still today, as His followers, we are feeding on Him in our hearts by faith. Jesus is the *Bread of Life*[5], and He satisfies our hunger for life and eternity. All temporal blessings as well as spiritual come from Him.

From the *Beginning*[6] we understand that Jesus existed as God from all eternity, in perfect fellowship with God the Father and with God the Holy Spirit.

> *Oh give thanks to the* LORD, *call upon His name* (1 Chronicles 16:8).

The Christian community is often challenged by atheists and skeptics to prove that there is a God because it is difficult for the natural man to believe in what he cannot see, touch, or feel. Yet the Bible clearly proclaims the existence of God and does not attempt to prove that He exists. Let us worship our Lord, Creator, and Savior, Jesus Christ, today and every day of our lives.

> *The Breath of the Almighty gives life to me.*
> *The Bridegroom, one day, I shall see.*
> *The Bread of Life is food for my soul,*
> *The Beginning and the End of all that I hold.*

Read the Scriptures below and write out specific ways to put the truths from today's reading into action in your own life. Refer to the *Personal Application Diary*.

[1] Job 33:4; [2] Zechariah 6:12; [3] Matthew 3:17; [4] Matthew 25:10; [5] John 6:35; [6] Revelation 21:6.

Personal Application Diary

Creator
Christ
Chief Corner Stone
Chosen One
Consuming Fire

4

There was a time when the Triune God dwelt alone. There was no heaven, no earth, no angels, and no universe. There was nothing, no one but God. He was and is complete in Himself. The Bible tells us that God created the heavens and the earth. He also created us and, as our *Creator*,[1] knows our needs in infinite detail. Since He is our Maker, we can entrust our lives to Him with complete confidence.

Christ is our Supreme Lord, since all things exist in, through, and for Him. His abundant grace is sufficient to see us through all the circumstances of life. The glory of *Christ*[2] is incomprehensible, His praises unutterable. Yet grace allows us the privilege to cry out, "Whom have I in heaven but You? And besides You, I desire nothing on earth" (Psalm 73:25).

God is at work building His Church with living stones. The *Chief Corner Stone*,[3] His Son, Jesus Christ, is the most important stone in God's building. He is what holds everything in place.

God has given us His *Chosen One*[4] as the supreme object of our faith and meditation—the fullest revelation of who and what God is, made manifest in the person of Christ.

We should remind ourselves that we cannot serve Him acceptably without due reverence for His majesty and His righteous anger. The faithfulness of God is a truth to be proclaimed not only when things are going well, but also when we suffer from His sharpest rebuke. The Lord knows what is best for each of us, and He is honored when, through trials and chastening, we recognize and acknowledge His love in His discipline.

For He is indeed a *Consuming Fire.*[5] When His rod falls on us, let us with David say, "I know, O LORD, that Your judgments are righteous, and that in faithfulness You have afflicted me" (Psalm 119:75).

> *"Blessed are You, O* LORD, *God of Israel our father... Both riches and honor come from You, and You rule over all, and in Your hand is power and might; and it lies in Your hand to make great and to strengthen everyone. Now therefore, our God, we thank You, and praise Your glorious name"* (1 Chronicles 29:10, 12-13).

The Author of Life knows our strengths, our weaknesses, our struggles, our joys. He longs to reveal Himself to us through His Son, Jesus Christ. Without the Chief Corner Stone, our lives would crumble. He knows our human frailties but is not interested in destroying us. If you have never done so before, invite Jesus Christ to come into your life. You'll discover that to know Him is to love Him. If you have already accepted Jesus Christ as your Lord and Savior, are you letting your light shine so that others may see the glory of God in you (Matthew 5:16)?

> *The Creator knows our every need,*
> *Fulfilled in Christ, the promised seed.*
> *The Chief Corner Stone is now in place;*
> *The Chosen One died for the whole human race.*

Read the Scriptures below and write out specific ways to put the truths from today's reading into action in your own life. Refer to the *Personal Application Diary.*

[1] Isaiah 40:28; [2] Matthew 16:16; [3] Mark 12:10; [4] Luke 23:35; [5] Hebrews 12:29.

Personal Application Diary

Everlasting God
Eternal Father
Everlasting Rock
Door of the Sheep
Deliverer
Eternal Spirit

5

$\mathfrak{T}$he *Everlasting God*,[1] our Eternal, Infinite Lord, has weighed us in His balance and found us lacking (Psalm 62:9). Yet, in the midst of our desperate situation, He draws us near to Himself because we are His children and He is *El-Olam*, "the Everlasting God," the *Eternal Father*.[2] The fatherhood of God is based not only on creation (our being born physically), but more importantly, on our being born spiritually. By God's grace, we become His children through faith in Jesus Christ. As His children, we are called to love, honor, respect, and obey Him, knowing that as our Father He will never leave us nor forsake us.

God has given us His names as a way to reveal His character. He cannot improve His character, because He is perfect. He cannot fail in any way, for the very same reason. Therefore, the absoluteness of the *Everlasting Rock*[3] is founded not on the strength of our resolutions or on our ability to persevere, but on the veracity of Him who cannot lie.

We are His sheep and He is the *Door of the Sheep*.[4] Jesus can be undoubtedly relied upon as the entrance to a personal relationship with God. Jesus said: "I am the way, and the truth, and the life; no one comes to the Father but through Me" (John 14:6).

As our *Deliverer*,[5] who surpasses the understanding of man, He meets us in every hour of need. Through the greatness of His compassion He rescues us from darkness and temptation and brings us to the light. He gives us hope when we have no hope. Our knowledge of God increases as we see Him fulfill all our needs. Yet we must not forget the mercy of God that delivered us from our sins, for without His love and mercy our lives would have no meaning.

God's *Eternal Spirit*,[6] equal with the Father and Son, replaces our blindness with the brightness of His presence. He calls us to serve in His kingdom by giving thanks in prosperity as well as in adversity.

> *"I have manifested Your name to the men whom You gave*
> *Me out of the world; they were Yours and You gave them to*
> *Me, and they have kept Your Word"* (John 17:6).

Our Everlasting Rock, our Deliverer, can and will carry us through each trial and temptation we face. God did not leave us without a Helper. Perhaps you fear that God could never forgive you and cleanse you from that secret sin. But nothing is beyond the reach of Christ's cleansing blood (1 John 1:7,9). Will you lay it before Him right now? His Eternal Spirit wants to remove the stain, remove the guilt, and renew a right spirit within you. Let us worship God for His work of grace in each of our lives.

> *On the Everlasting Rock I shall stand;*
> *The Door of the Sheep is in command.*
> *My Deliverer placed me in His light;*
> *In the Eternal Spirit there is no night.*

Read the Scriptures below and write out specific ways to put the truths from today's reading into action in your own life. Refer to the *Personal Application Diary.*

[1] Genesis 21:33; [2] Isaiah 9:6; [3] Isaiah 26:4; [4] John 10:7; [5] Galatians 1:4; [6] Hebrews 9:14.

Personal Application Diary

Father
Father of Our Lord Jesus Christ
Father of Mercies
Father of Glory
Faithful
Father of Lights

6

God has revealed Himself as *Father*.[1] As such, He loves, protects, and provides for His children. He is the source of believers' spiritual lives and pours out His love upon them. He is concerned with their welfare (Romans 8:28) as well as with their discipline (Hebrews 12:5).

Through the name *Father of Our Lord Jesus Christ*,[2] God reveals Himself as the first person in the Trinity, having a unique relationship with Christ. Every attribute of God that is revealed individually through one of His names is brought together collectively in the person of the Son: "For it was the Father's good pleasure for all the fullness to dwell in Him" (Colossians 1:19).

As the *Father of Mercies*,[3] He is sensitive to our every need. We can rest on Him in every trial. His preserving, sustaining, and pardoning mercies are unending.

As the *Father of Glory*,[4] He is magnificent. One day He will transform our suffering into glory. He can be glorified even in circumstances that to us look like tragedy.

God's Word of promise is true and sure. In all His relations with His people He is *Faithful*.[5] This title connotes a quality that is essential to His being. Without it He would not be God. In Deuteronomy 7:9 we read, "Know therefore that the LORD your God, He is God, the faithful God, who keeps His covenant and His lovingkindness to a thousandth generation with those who love Him and keep His commandments." God's promise to be faithful is the heart of His relationship with men. That is, He is faithful in all things and faithful at all times. He is trustworthy and righteous. He is faithful in what He withholds, as well as in what He gives.

Light dispels darkness, and as the *Father of Lights*,[6] nothing is hidden from Him (Hebrews 4:13). Whatever He has decreed will come to pass. God does not want to keep us in darkness. He gave us the Bible as a lamp to show us the way so that we may walk in the light.

> *"Naked I came from my mother's womb, and naked I shall return there. The LORD gave and the LORD has taken away. Blessed be the name of the LORD"* (Job 1:21).

We are living in a time when unfaithfulness is one of the most prevalent failures of our day. None of us is immune. "For all have sinned and fall short of the glory of God" (Romans 3:23). How often have we been unfaithful to Christ and to our fellow men and women? How often have we been unfaithful in the use of the resources He has entrusted to us? Let us be faithful as He is faithful.

> *O, what a Faithful God is He,*
> *The Father of Lights for all to see.*
> *Faithful and True is His name.*
> *My loving Father, forever the same.*

Read the Scriptures below and write out specific ways to put the truths from today's reading into action in your own life. Refer to the *Personal Application Diary*.

[1] Jeremiah 3:19; [2,3] 2 Corinthians 1:3; [4] Ephesians 1:17; [5] Hebrews 10:23; [6] 2 Corinthians 4:6; [7] Hebrews 4:13.

Personal Application Diary

God Who Sees
God of Hosts
God of Heaven
God of All the Earth
God Who Is Near
Great God

7

God is the all-powerful Creator who keeps His promises. The Hebrew word for God, *Elohim*, refers to God's deity, power, and might. He is above all, sustains all, and is independent of all. He cannot be known by human wisdom.

Through the psalmist, God complained to an apostate Israel, "These things you have done and I kept silence; you thought that I was just like you; I will reprove you" (Psalm 50:21). God's warning to Israel is appropriate for our generation. Meditating upon the infinite knowledge of God should motivate us to act with maturity. He is incomparable and worthy of our worship. Nothing is hidden from Him because He is the *God Who Sees*.[1] *El-Ro'i* is Hebrew for "the Strong One who sees."

As the *God of Hosts*[2] He is the commander in chief of the army of heaven. Angels are at His command to be bearers of His messages and guardians of His people.

Heaven is a place where there is no sin, hunger, or thirst; a place where there is no death, pain, sickness, or tears; a place of holiness, beauty, perfection, and joy. The *God of Heaven*[3] knows all and has sovereign command over everything in heaven, on earth, and under the earth. Whatever the LORD pleases, He does (Psalm 135:6).

He is *God of All the Earth*.[4] Our lives are neither the product of fate nor of chance. Every detail has been ordained by our living and reigning God.

We are cautioned against putting our hope or trust in human beings.

"Do not trust in princes, in mortal man, in whom there is no salvation" (Psalm 146:3). We cannot rely on mortal men, because they are forever changing, but we can place our trust in God who is unchanging. Remember, the heroes of today often become the has-beens of tomorrow.

He is the *God Who Is Near*[5] and the God who longs to have intimate communion with His children. When God seems far away, it is we who have strayed, not He. Too often, we focus on either the past or the future and fail to see that the Lord is working in our lives *today*. He is the *Great God* [6] who is majestic and worthy of our worship and adoration.

> *Let not the oppressed return dishonored; let the afflicted and*
> *needy praise Your name* (Psalm 74:21).

We are precious in God's sight and therefore we cannot escape the scrutiny of His watchful eyes. He is never so far from us that we cannot cry out to him. There is no tear that He does not see. There is no cry that He cannot hear. There is no problem He cannot solve. As we trust and give reverence to Him, we can expect Him to guide us in the difficult decisions of everyday life.

> *Elohim, in His creation was well pleased.*
> *El-Ro'i, nothing hidden from the God who sees.*
> *As the God of Hosts His people need not fear.*
> *We have intimate fellowship with our God Who Is Near.*

Read the Scriptures below and write out specific ways to put the truths from today's reading into action in your own life. Refer to the *Personal Application Diary.*

[1] Genesis 16:13; [2] Psalm 89:8; [3] Psalm 136:26; [4] Isaiah 54:5; [5] Jeremiah 23:23; [6] Titus 2:13.

Personal Application Diary

God of Your Fathers
God of the Hebrews
God of Jerusalem
God of Jacob
God of Abraham
God of Israel
God of Daniel
God of Isaac

8

The *God of Your Fathers*[1] is the One our ancestors worshiped. The Bible pictures Him as loving and approachable.

After the fall of Adam and Eve, mankind plunged into sin and evil. Subsequently, God destroyed the earth by flood, but arranged for Noah and his family to survive. Even the judgment of the flood failed to stem the tide of depravity. As a result, God turned to a specific people, the Hebrews. The *God of the Hebrews*[2] is the Sovereign Lord of the people.

The *God of Jerusalem*[3] is the God of a royal city; the City of David; the holy city; the city of the Great King; the city of God; the capital of the only physical kingdom God has established among men. God reigns forever in the hearts of those who choose to follow Him. He is coming again to establish His eternal kingdom.

The *God of Jacob*[4] is the Faithful Lord of Israel. The remnant of Israel, which still holds to the promises of God regarding the Messiah, will one day confess that the rejected and despised One, whom their fathers delivered into the hands of the Gentiles, is the Son of God, the King of Israel.

The nation of Israel came into being because of the obedience of one man, Abraham. God called Abraham out of the land of Ur of the Chaldees. Abraham heard and responded to God's call. *The God of Abraham*[5] is

Abraham's Lord and our God. He gave Abraham the promise and its fulfillment.

The *God of Israel*[6] is the leader of His people, "Blessed be the LORD God, the God of Israel, who alone works wonders" (Psalm 72:18).

The *God of Daniel*[7] is the God whom Daniel served. Daniel knew that His God could deliver him from the lion's den.

The *God of Isaac*[8] is the God who keeps His promises, for it was through Isaac that God's covenant with Israel was fulfilled. In a Jewish setting, God's link with the patriarchs would show that His present nature was recognized as identical to the God who dealt graciously with the fathers of the Jewish race.

> *So the nations will fear the name of the LORD, and all the kings of the earth Your glory* (Psalm 102:15).

Through Isaiah the prophet, God declared, "Therefore the Lord Himself will give you a sign: Behold, a virgin will be with child and bear a son, and she will call His name Immanuel" (Isaiah 7:14). Again, the promises of God are true. Many centuries later, the God of our fathers became flesh: "But when the fullness of the time came, God sent forth His Son, born of a woman, born under the Law" (Galatians 4:4). *Immanuel* literally means "God with us." What a wonderful reality!

> *The God of Jerusalem established His kingdom among men.*
> *The God of the Hebrews delivers His people from sin.*
> *The God of Our Fathers is faithful and true.*
> *The God of Your Fathers, our ancestors worshiped, too.*

Read the Scriptures below and write out specific ways to put the truths from today's reading into action in your own life. Refer to the *Personal Application Diary.*

[1] Exodus 3:13; [2] Exodus 5:3; [3] Ezra 7:19; [4] Psalm 46:11; [5] Psalm 47:9; [6] Isaiah 21:10; [7] Daniel 6:26; [8] Matthew 22:32.

Personal Application Diary

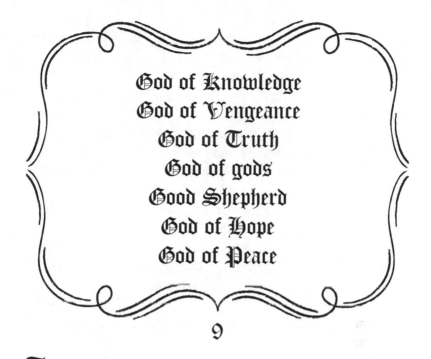

God of Knowledge
God of Vengeance
God of Truth
God of gods
Good Shepherd
God of Hope
God of Peace

9

𝕿he *God of Knowledge*[1] knows everything about the past, the present, and the future. He knows every detail about the life of every human being. He knows our thoughts, words, deeds, needs, sorrows, and frailties. We bow in awe and adoration of the One from whom nothing can be concealed. With the psalmist we proclaim, "Such knowledge is too wonderful for me; it is too high, I cannot attain to it" (Psalm 139:6). We may not understand fully all that God plans for us, but we know that He never makes a mistake. He knows our needs, and He knows what is best. "But He knows the way I take; when He has tried me, I shall come forth as gold" (Job 23:10).

Our Lord is not ashamed to make it known that He is a *God of Vengeance*[2] who punishes evil. The more we reflect upon God's abhorrence of sin and His vengeance upon it, the more we should serve Him with reverence and godly fear. Daily we need to make certain that we are in harmony with Him. The *God of Truth*[3] is righteous and accurate: "Behold, You desire truth in the innermost being, and in the hidden part You will make me know wisdom" (Psalm 51:6). Knowing the truth will set us free.

The *God of gods*[4] knows and foreknows all things. He will have the last word in the destiny of every man. Neither men nor angels shall be able to thwart His plan.

Jesus is the *Good Shepherd*[5] who came into the world, braving hardship and peril, to seek and save His lost sheep. This title connotes the great value Jesus places on people as it speaks of His willingness to suffer and die to save even only one lost sheep.

How encouraging it is to know that when the world hates us, God loves us. He loved us when we were unlovely. Our security, therefore, is in Him, the *God of Hope*.[6] Some people believe that Christians are not supposed to experience pain and bereavement, but that is not the case. Still, God does not want us to grieve "as do the rest who have no hope" (1 Thessalonians 4:13).

In a world of strife and turmoil, the *God of Peace*[7] offers stability and victory to those who earnestly seek Him.

> *He restores my soul; He guides me in the paths of righteousness for His name's sake* (Psalm 23:3).

When the Good Shepherd directs His sheep, He goes before them and prepares the way. He knows the winding paths of life and what lies ahead of us. Our tomorrows are already in His mind and heart. We have nothing to worry about since the Lord, who is our Shepherd, is committed to seeing us through. What a source of confidence and strength when we experience weakness and doubt!

> *God of Knowledge, too wonderful for me;*
> *God of Truth, who set us free;*
> *God of all comfort, compassionate is He;*
> *God of Peace gives us stability.*

Read the Scriptures below and write out specific ways to put the truths from today's reading into action in your own life. Refer to the *Personal Application Diary*.

[1] 1 Samuel 2:3; [2] Psalm 94:1; [3] Isaiah 65:16; [4] Daniel 2:47; [5] John 10:11; [6] Romans 15:13; [7] 1 Thessalonians 5:23.

Personal Application Diary

Holy One of Israel
Helper
Healer
High and Exalted One
Holy

10

Regardless of whether He is recognized as such, the fact remains that Jesus is the pure, divine head of the nation of Israel. He is the *Holy One of Israel.*[1]

As our *Helper,*[2] He sustains us in our sorrow, comforts us when we are sad, gives us strength when we are weary, dries our tears, and gives us hope. When we feel threatened, we can cry out, "The LORD is my helper, I will not be afraid. What will man do to me?" (Hebrews 13:6).

The toll which sickness has exacted upon human life and happiness is tragic and costly. Every day we are confronted with the reality that sickness is not a respecter of persons. We do not only experience physical pain, but we sometimes experience pain caused by broken relationships. Jesus, who is the *Healer*[3] (*Jehovah-Rapha*, "the God who heals"), is not only capable of healing our physical ailments but also our disappointments and shattered hopes and dreams. He identifies with each of His children because he is "a man of sorrows and acquainted with grief" (Isaiah 53:3). He knows how we feel, and He shares His comfort with us. He has entered into our pain and sorrow and will ultimately use seeming tragedy for our good and for His glory. To the sick, God's Word says, "The LORD will sustain him upon his sickbed; in his illness, You restore him to health" (Psalm 41:3). To those crushed in spirit because of a broken relationship, God offers His peace.

The God above all is the *High and Exalted One:*[4] "Set your mind on the things above, not on the things that are on earth" (Colossians 3:2).

One of the most distinct qualities of God in the Old Testament is His holiness. Holiness marks Him out as being totally pure in thought and attitude. God is *Holy*[5] and we are called to be like Him. We have to live in the world but not be followers of the world. We have to live in contact with the world, but we do not have to be contaminated by it.

> *"Father, glorify Your name." Then a voice came out of heaven: "I have both glorified it, and will glorify it again"* (John 12:28).

Through holy living we become the salt of the earth. Holy living begins by asking Jesus to saturate every area of our lives with the transforming power of His Spirit. We are called to influence the world and not be infected by it. Holiness is what God is, and as we seek to grow in holiness, we become more and more like Him. The process of having our faith tested in everyday human experience is not always pleasant, but we have hope in knowing that our lives will increasingly reflect the beauty of holiness to the eternal glory of God.

> *With our Helper, we shall not be afraid.*
> *Through the Holy One of Israel a foundation has been laid.*
> *Jehovah-Rapha, our Healer is He.*
> *High and Exalted One, help us keep our eyes on Thee.*

Read the Scriptures below and write out specific ways to put the truths from today's reading into action in your own life. Refer to the *Personal Application Diary*.

[1] 2 Kings 19:22; [2] Psalm 54:4; [3] Isaiah 53:5; [4] Isaiah 57:15; [5] Luke 1:49.

Personal Application Diary

Heavenly Father
Holy One
Holy Spirit
Head of the Church
High Priest

11

Our *Heavenly Father*[1] is perfect, holy, personal, and compassionate. As a child enjoys the privilege of running into his father's presence at any time, so can the believer approach God's presence with boldness and confidence, knowing that the Father will hear him.

He is the *Holy One*[2] who, despite His love for His Son, Jesus Christ, did not withhold His wrath from Him. God abhors sin, but He loves us so much that He willingly gave His Son to die on the cross for our sin.

The *Holy Spirit*[3] is the third person of the Godhead and is present in us. True faith must always center on Christ, through whom God reconciled the world unto Himself. It is the Holy Spirit who makes God personal to each of us by uniting us to Christ. He is likened to a dove, which is gentle, and to the unseen mysterious forces of the wind. Like the wind He moves mysteriously through the natural world and through the spiritual realms. He is the Comforter who guides and directs our Christian lives.

With Christ as the *Head of the Church*,[4] we are eternally secure in our present spiritual state of transformation by His saving grace.

The book of Hebrews was written to Jewish Christians who were tempted to renounce Jesus Christ and return to Judaism. The writer of Hebrews, therefore, demonstrates the supremacy of Christ. He demonstrates that the sacrificial ministry of Jesus Christ is incomparably superior to the now obsolete Levitical priesthood. As our *High Priest*,[5] Jesus is the only mediator between God and mankind. At this very moment, Jesus is in heaven praying for His people. He is our faithful High Priest, and He ever lives to make intercession for us (Hebrews 7:25). He is interceding for us at this very moment, just when we need Him most.

> *"Pray, then, in this way: 'Our Father who is in heaven, hallowed be Your name.'"* (Matthew 6:9).

In God's eyes, every person is important. He sent His only Son to die for us. May we remember with gratitude what a privilege it is to have a Father in heaven to whom we can go at any time and not feel that we are intruders. Our Father's love knows no bounds. The Church is His bride, and He is coming again in glory and power. As one songwriter in the 1950s put it, "Our God is big enough to control the universe, but can still reside in my heart."

Let us be ready to meet our Bridegroom.

> *Heavenly Father, I praise Your Son.*
> *His name is Jesus, the Holy One,*
> *Head of the Church who died in my place,*
> *Holy Spirit sent by Your grace.*

Read the Scriptures below and write out specific ways to put the truths from today's reading into action in your own life. Refer to the *Personal Application Diary.*

[1] Luke 11:13; [2] Proverbs 9:10; [3] 1 Corinthians 6:19; [4] Ephesians 5:23; [5] Hebrews 4:14.

Personal Application Diary

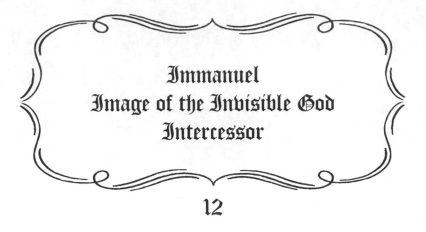

Immanuel
Image of the Invisible God
Intercessor

12

God's nature and being are infinite. There never was a time when He was not, and there never will be a time when He ceases to be. He is the witness, not only of the past and the future, but of the truth itself. As such, He describes Himself as the *I AM*.[1] This name speaks of Him as being self-existing, self-determining, eternal, unchanging, and sovereign. He is not the "I was" or "I will be" but the I AM. He is the underlying cause of all events, the reality behind reality. God is completely free from constraint and dependence upon anything outside Himself.

Every year brings with it a fresh witness to God's fulfillment of His promises. Isaiah declared, "Therefore the Lord Himself will give you a sign: Behold, a virgin will be with child and bear a son, and she will call His name *Immanuel*."[2] And after many centuries passed, "when the fullness of the time came, God sent forth His Son, born of a woman, born under the Law" (Galatians 4:4). His word of promise is sure, for indeed, God is with us in the presence of His Son, Jesus.

Jesus is the *Image of the Invisible God*.[3] The Bible makes it clear that every believer is involved in a spiritual battle (Galatians 5:17) and that God's plan for our spiritual maturity involves a continuing process of change toward Christ-likeness (Romans 8:29). We can expect Him to demonstrate His perfection through our personalities just as God demonstrated His perfection through the life of Jesus Christ almost two thousand years ago. Jesus will do in us whatever His nature moves Him to do, unless He is hindered by our own stubborn human will.

Right now, Jesus Christ, our *Intercessor*,[4] is praying for us. He knows when we are faced with criticism, fear, pain, pressure, resentment, hurts, and unanswered questions—all part of the painful reality and consequence of living as imperfect beings in an imperfect, sinful world. He will not allow us to be tempted beyond what we can bear (1 Corinthians 10:13). He gives us the victory in every temptation, trial, or problem.

> *"... and I have made Your name known to them, and will make it known, so that the love with which You loved Me may be in them, and I in them"* (John 17:26).

Isn't it encouraging to know that our Intercessor is there for us during difficult and stressful times? Let us be reminded that "the Spirit also helps our weakness; for we do not know how to pray as we should, but the Spirit Himself intercedes for us" (Romans 8:26). Have we been faithful in interceding for people in difficult situations? Our prayers can make a difference!

> *Gracious Intercessor who prays for me,*
> *Image of the Invisible God I will one day see.*
> *The great I AM will never leave me alone;*
> *Immanuel is coming back for His very own.*

Read the Scriptures below and write out specific ways to put the truths from today's reading into action in your own life. Refer to the *Personal Application Diary.*

[1] Exodus 3:14; [2] Isaiah 7:14; [3] Colossians 1:15; [4] Hebrews 7:25.

Personal Application Diary

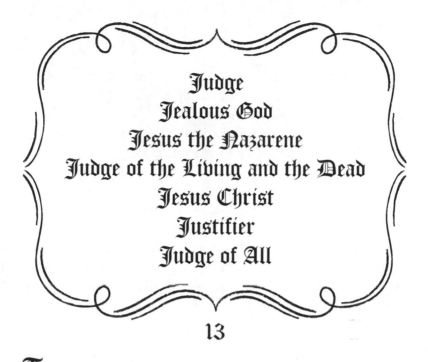

Judge
Jealous God
Jesus the Nazarene
Judge of the Living and the Dead
Jesus Christ
Justifier
Judge of All

13

𝕿he Bible declares again and again that God is *Judge*.[1] As He did with Adam and Eve, with Israel, and with the world before the flood, He inflicts judgment on those who deserve it. Let us be mindful that He is grieved when His people are disobedient. He is also pained by the destruction sin brings with it.

Our Lord is revealed as a *Jealous God*[2] because He has a righteous zeal. He cannot and will not tolerate being worshiped along with other gods. We are called to renounce all things or people we have loved, sought, or placed ahead of God: our work, our family, our leisure, our possessions, ourselves. We are called to renounce the use of images. Those who use images in worship eventually take their theology from them. The Bible makes it clear that "those who make them will be like them, yes, everyone who trusts in them" (Psalm 135:18). The image-worshiper tends to neglect God's revealed will. The mind taken up with images is a mind that has not yet learned to love and obey God's Word alone. Has God and His Word replaced the images in our lives?

The region of Nazareth in the days of Christ was held in contempt (John 1:46), but this was the home of *Jesus the Nazarene*,[3] whose sinless life was such a contrast to the citizens of that place. Jesus is also the *Judge of the*

Living and the Dead[4] and has final authority over all human beings—over you and me.

Jesus Christ[5] is fully God and at the same time fully man, yet He did not sin. God, out of His abundant grace, determined to give His Son as a ransom for sinners. Jesus Christ is the perfect sacrifice, without blemish, who died that we might have life. Christ did not die in order for God to love us, but He died *because* God loves us. God never sends man to hell. Man makes his own choice to go to hell when he rejects the *Justifier,*[6] Jesus Christ. We who are His children, however, can rest in the fact that no one can bring a charge against us, for God alone is the One who justifies.

Jesus is the *Judge of All.*[7] No one is exempt from His judgment. When we are tempted at times to question God's justice when we see evil men prosper, let us take heart and say, "And He will judge the world in righteousness; He will execute judgment for the peoples with equity" (Psalm 9:8). God is on our side.

> *... and for the Gentiles to glorify God for His mercy; as it is written, "Therefore I will give praise to You among the Gentiles, and I will sing to Your name"* (Romans 15:9).

Jesus had every reason to choose not to die for us. Yet He who knew no sin humbly accepted the sufferings of the cross in order that we might have eternal life. Are we ready to make an account of our lives to Jesus, the Righteous Judge?

> *God is Judge; oh, may the world see*
> *That the Jealous God had mercy on me.*
> *Judge of the Living and of the Dead,*
> *The Judge of All will have the last word when all is said.*

Read the Scriptures below and write out specific ways to put the truths from today's reading into action in your own life. Refer to the *Personal Application Diary.*

[1] Genesis 18:25; [2] Exodus 20:5; [3] John 18:5; [4] Acts 10:42; [5] Romans 3:22; [6] Romans 8:33; [7] Hebrews 12:23.

Personal Application Diary

King of Glory
King over all the Earth
King of the Nations
King of Heaven
King of the Jews
King Eternal
King of kings

14

The glory of God is something we can never fully describe or experience here on earth. As we reflect on God's glory, we are drawn to worship Him for the divine splendor and majesty attached to His revelation of Himself and to the praise and honor He alone deserves. Our awesome majesty is the *King of Glory*[1] who has authority over all the world and is the *King over all the Earth*.[2] Let us not be discouraged by the tactics of Satan, for he has already been judged.

God is sovereign over all governments and peoples because He is the *King of the Nations*.[3] All nations, kings, and princes are subject to Him. They derive their authority from Him. As citizens of this earth, we are commanded to submit ourselves to the governing authorities. When we do this, we subject ourselves also to the King of the Nations.

God sits on the throne as the *King of Heaven*.[4] We proclaim both the King and His kingship over all the works of His hands and the throne of God and His right to sit upon that throne. We extol God's right to do as He pleases with His creatures without consulting them.

Jesus Christ, who was initially rejected by the nation, Israel, is none other than the *King of the Jews*.[5] His earthly kingdom is only a shadow of the good things to come. Throughout the ages, God has revealed the way by which man can return to Him. The "times" and "seasons" of this world are the shadows of those "ages," for He is the *King Eternal*.[6]

God exercises His sovereignty according to His own desires. He has mercy on whom He wills, and He hardens whom He wills. Our lives and all that we possess are held at His disposal. Whatever the Lord pleases, He does. He is above all rulers and therefore is the *King of kings*.[7] All principalities and powers are subject to Him. He is worthy of our adoration and worship.

> *Through Him then, let us continually offer up a sacrifice of praise to God, that is, the fruit of lips that give thanks to His name* (Hebrews 13:15).

We shall behold His glory when we see Him face-to-face. We shall bow down in adoration of the King of Glory and the King of kings. Every tongue will declare Him as the Lord, but need we wait for that time to come? Right now, let us offer up a song of praise to our King Eternal. He is the King of the Jews, but He is also our King who sits on the throne of our hearts. Let His majesty and dominion endure forever and ever.

> *Our awesome majesty is the King of Glory.*
> *O King over all the Earth, we live to tell Your story.*
> *You are the King Eternal no matter how it seems;*
> *One day the world will know that You are the King of kings.*

Read the Scriptures below and write out specific ways to put the truths from today's reading into action in your own life. Refer to the *Personal Application Diary*.

[1] Psalm 24:8; [2] Psalm 47:2; [3] Jeremiah 10:7; [4] Daniel 4:37; [5] Matthew 27:11; [6] 1 Timothy 1:17; [7] 1 Timothy 6:15.

Personal Application Diary

Lamb of God
Lawgiver
Love
Lion that is from the Tribe of Judah

15

The *Lamb of God*[1] is God's provision for our sins. Jesus is the true Lamb of God who takes away the sins of the world. If we desire to see the Father, we must focus on His Son: "Behold the Lamb."

The day is coming when the *Lawgiver*[2] will make an awesome display of His wrath. He will take vengeance upon all who oppose His laws. Those who have not surrendered their lives to Jesus Christ as Lord and Savior are still in their sins and on the way to everlasting death. To the Christian, He is a tender Father under the new covenant of grace, yet He will not allow sin in our lives to go without rebuke. To the rebellious lawbreaker, He will yet be a consuming fire. Those who reject Him will suffer in a place of unquenchable fire—a place of misery, pain, separation, and wrath. Faithfulness demands that we speak as passionately about hell as we do about heaven.

The Bible proclaims that God is *Love*.[3] The declaration is not simply that God loves, but rather that He *is* love. His very nature is that of love. The cross of Calvary is the supreme demonstration of His love. The love of God does not forsake sinful man. His Spirit continues to strive with man even in his state of utter corruption. Sadly, many today talk about the love of God, yet they do not know the God of love personally. John the Baptist pointed to Jesus as the Lamb of God who takes away the sins of the world. How often we beat our chest in remorse and say, "Lamb of God who takes away the sins of the world, have mercy on me," and still not have the assurance of eternal life simply because we have not made Jesus our personal Lord and Savior! Let us take time, if we have never done so, to say, "Jesus is the

Lamb of God who has taken away my sins." The miracle of God's love is that it transcends age, culture, religion, and tradition.

Although He is the Lamb, we must never forget that He is also the Lion. He is the *Lion that is from the Tribe of Judah*[4] who has irresistible strength and power. The Lamb and the Lion are both demonstrations of God's love and mercy.

> *Now when He was in Jerusalem at the Passover, during the feast, many believed in His name, beholding His signs which He was doing* (John 2:23).

No matter how far away God may seem to you today, no matter how hard your heart may be, Jesus loves you. The tenderest of all God's personal attributes is love. Love is what God is, not just something He does. Some people love in order to take. God loves in order to give. He loved the world He knew would not love Him back—a world that chose to rebel against Him. May God grant us the grace to trust His timing, claim His promises, and rest in His love.

> *Oh, divine Lawgiver who obeyed the Law for us;*
> *Lamb of God, God's provision in whom we place our trust;*
> *Lion that is from the Tribe of Judah, irresistible in strength and power;*
> *God of Love, we praise Your name—each and every hour.*

Read the Scriptures below and write out specific ways to put the truths from today's reading into action in your own life. Refer to the *Personal Application Diary*.

[1] John 1:29; [2] James 4:12; [3] 1 John 4:8; [4] Revelation 5:5.

Personal Application Diary

Lily of the Valleys
Leader
Light
Life
Lamb

16

Our physical lives can be sustained without beautiful flowers to delight our eyes with color and our noses with sweet smells. We can live our lives without walking through fields, listening to the soothing singing of birds. Yet it is natural for us to appreciate beautiful things because they add color and zest to our lives. However, this beauty pales in comparison to the splendor and glory of the *Lily of the Valleys*.[1]

God is our supreme commander, our *Leader*,[2] who calls us to walk in the light. When the darkness of sin clouds our perception of God, let us run to our Leader and ask Him to illumine our hearts so that we can see beyond ourselves.

Where *Light*[3] shines, darkness is dispelled, revealing the true nature of man. In this world darkened by sin and unbelief, man has fallen, yet God's light still illumines man's path to true salvation and to the everlasting arms of God. Jesus is the perfect light in whose radiance all other lights grow dim.

All things and all men owe their existence to the *Life*[4] of God in Christ. He alone is the source of eternal life. When all is lost in darkness and confusion, He first brings back His light and life, and then His image. He makes all things new. Nothing hinders His work or changes His purpose.

The Jews were familiar with the meaning of the word *Lamb*,[5] because lambs were used as the sacrifice to cleanse them from their sins. Jesus is now the Perfect Lamb who shed His blood once and for all time to save us from our sins. Sacrifice cannot be separated from the Lamb. With the blood of Jesus covering us, we now have the power to offer our minds, our wills, and our emotions to God.

> But as many as received Him, to them He gave the right to become children of God, even to those who believed in His name (John 1:12).

Praise God that the transforming power of the Holy Spirit offers a personal passion and inner power to please the One who has set us free. We will behold Him one day fully, but we experience His beauty in part now. Let us not allow God's beauty and glory to be overshadowed by temporal things.

> Lily of the Valleys, what beauty to behold,
> Changing by His Life as each day unfolds,
> Yielding mind, will, and emotions to the Lamb, ever to be a fight;
> Victory won only as we walk in His Light.

Read the Scriptures below and write out specific ways to put the truths from today's reading into action in your own life. Refer to the *Personal Application Diary*.

[1] Song of Solomon 2:1; [2] Matthew 23:10; [3] John 8:12; [4] John 11:25; [5] Revelation 5:6.

Personal Application Diary

**Lord Will Provide
Lord of Hosts
Last Adam
Lord Almighty
Lord of Peace
Lord of lords
Living God**

17

Abraham referred to God as *Jehovah-Jireh* or the LORD *Will Provide*.[1] Just as God provided a ram as a substitute for Abraham's only son, Isaac (Genesis 22:1-14), He has provided His only Son, Jesus Christ, as the sacrifice for those bound by sin. It is only through Christ that we can come into the righteous and holy presence of God. In every age, the LORD *of Hosts*[2] has been the rest, refuge, and comfort of His people. He is also the captain of the army of heaven.

Adam, the father of all mankind, rebelled against God. After he sinned, he hid himself from God and tried to cover what he had done. He also tried to excuse his rebellion. This story is re-enacted every day as man lives according to the nature of Adam. As the *Last Adam*,[3] Jesus is different from Adam and his descendants. There was nothing in Him that yielded to sin or Satan. In Christ we are called to renounce all features and manifestations of self-life such as: a secret pride in success; good training; appearance; natural abilities; a self-important, independent spirit; an attitude that says, "my way is best, and I'm always right"; a love of human praise; a secret yearning to be noticed; love of supremacy; a need to draw attention to self in conversation; stirrings of anger and impatience; a tendency to resent correction and retaliate when contradicted; and a desire to throw sharp, heated remarks at others. These are but a few examples of the life we have inherited from the First Adam. Praise be to God that the remedy for man's being lost is found in the Last Adam! God's image is restored in us by the indwelling presence of the Last Adam, Jesus Christ.

He is the awesome, all-powerful *Lord Almighty*.[4] As the *Lord of Peace*,[5] He brings security and comfort to those who trust Him and choose to obey Him. Because *Jehovah-Shalom*, "the LORD is peace," loves us, He wants to bless us with His peace that passes all understanding (Philippians 4:7). Only His peace is lasting in a world of turmoil where there is a famine of peace.

As the *Lord of lords*,[6] He is the greatest of all, the Ruler of rulers. As the *Living God*,[7] He is the Lord of life who is alive forever and has sovereign control over everything that happens in our lives.

> *All who are under the yoke as slaves are to regard their own*
> *masters as worthy of all honor so that the name of God and*
> *our doctrine will not be spoken against* (1 Timothy 6:1).

As weak and fallen as His creatures are, the Lord of All calls us to the closest and most endearing communion with Himself. He is the Sovereign Owner of everything, yet He has given Himself to us that we might give ourselves to Him. "With all my heart I have sought You; do not let me wander from Your commandments" (Psalm 119:10).

> *Jehovah-Jireh, the LORD Will Provide.*
> *Captain of the army of heaven, LORD of Hosts at our side;*
> *The Last Adam—remedy for man's sin;*
> *Lord of lords, Ruler of rulers, yet my intimate friend.*

Read the Scriptures below and write out specific ways to put the truths from today's reading into action in your own life. Refer to the *Personal Application Diary.*

[1] Genesis 22:14; [2] Psalm 24:10; [3] 1 Corinthians 15:45-47; [4] 2 Corinthians 6:18; [5] 2 Thessalonians 3:16; [6] 1 Timothy 6:15; [7] Hebrews 3:12.

Personal Application Diary

Most High
Mighty One of Israel
Maker of All
Mighty God
Messiah

18

The biblical writers used height as a symbol of transcendence, just as we do. When thinking of the *Most High*,[1] we are called to look upward rather than downward, and outside rather than inside ourselves. The name Most High reveals the relationship God has with all His creation, even to the world outside the elect. In Hebrew, *El Elyon* is generally considered to be one of the most ancient names for God in the Old Testament. This name connotes supreme dignity, which expresses the superiority of God over all other gods. Even through judgment He will carry out His own purpose in each of our lives. There is no one greater.

The transcendence of the true and living God might well be challenged by mankind because of the infinite distance that separates the Creator from His creation. Yet the infinite God manifested Himself to the nation of Israel with the love of a father. The powerful Sovereign of the universe is the *Mighty One of Israel*.[2]

As *Maker of All*[3] He is the One who controls the destiny of all men. Yet He did not leave us without a solution to our sin problem. The New Testament affirms that the infinite God became man. At the cross, Jesus disarmed and triumphed over the devil and all principalities and powers by His command. The decisive defeat of Satan took place at the cross. The ultimate crushing of Satan is accomplished by our *Mighty God*,[4] the all-powerful Ruler of the universe.

The popular Messianic expectation of the Jewish nation was that of a revolutionary political leader. But Jesus declared, "For even the Son of

Man did not come to be served, but to serve, and to give His life a ransom for many" (Mark 10:45). This example demonstrates that the ransom for our freedom is nothing less than the Anointed One of God. The rejected and despised One is the *Messiah*,[5] the Son of God, the King of Israel. He did not cling to the privileges of His status, of equality with God. Instead, He went to the cross in self-denial and complete obedience to fulfill His destiny as God's Messiah.

> *"For the Mighty One has done great things for me; and holy is His name"* (Luke 1:49).

God's faithfulness was revealed to the nation of Israel by means of a covenant requiring the shedding of the blood of animals. As partakers of the new covenant, we understand that the Old Testament animal blood sacrifices are now obsolete. Christ's atonement for our sin was accomplished on the cross. The curtain that once separated us from God has been torn down. Great is the love of our Father who gave us His Son that we might also become heirs to His promise of eternal life. Praise His holy name!

> *O, Most High God, there is no one greater.*
> *Maker of All, our loving Creator,*
> *Messiah, King of Israel will not abandon*
> *Or leave His people alone.*
> *Our Sovereign and Mighty God is on His throne.*

Read the Scriptures below and write out specific ways to put the truths from today's reading into action in your own life. Refer to the *Personal Application Diary.*

[1] Psalm 46:4; [2] Isaiah 1:24; [3] Jeremiah 10:16; [4] Isaiah 9:6; [5] John 1:41.

Personal Application Diary

Only One
One
Name Which Is Above Every Name
Mediator
Omega

19

Do we worship the *Only One*?[1] Here is the test: God has spoken through His Son. Do we look continually to the person and work of Jesus Christ to show us the final truth about the character and grace of God? Do we see all the purposes of God as centering upon Him? If, by God's grace, we see this and cling to the cross as God's solution to our sin, we can know that we worship the one and only true God and have eternal life. "And this is eternal life, that they may know You, the only true God, and Jesus Christ whom You have sent" (John 17:3).

Jesus is the *One*,[2] for He has a unique relationship with God the Father. In the majesty of the Trinity there is a plurality in the Godhead. Christ has a very special relationship with the Father and with the Holy Spirit. Since He is God, this relationship can never be broken.

Clothed with the armor of God, we can take our stand against the devil, and he will flee because Jesus defeated him at the cross. Yet our own feeble voice is not authoritative enough to make him flee. We must dismiss him in the name of Jesus Christ. He flees before the *Name Which Is Above Every Name*.[3] The King of kings is reigning in the universe. Yet He is also waiting until His enemies become a footstool for His feet. On that day, every knee will bow to Him and every tongue will confess He is Lord.

It is through Christ the *Mediator*[4] alone that the grace of God flows to His elect. Immortality belongs to God's essential being and therefore He cannot die. Neither does death have any hold on those who are His children. Jesus became man in order to free us from the power of death (Hebrews 2:14).

Completeness in this day and age is sometimes equated with having a husband, children, and a good education, or with being successful in one's profession. This description has led many to strive for the stars, no matter what the cost. At the end, however, there is still no hope, no fulfillment. How blessed are those whose eyes are fixed on the *Omega*,[5] for He is the ultimate of everything—our reason for being.

> O LORD, our Lord, how majestic is Your name in all
> the earth, who have displayed Your splendor above the
> heavens! ...O LORD, our Lord, how majestic is Your name
> in all the earth! (Psalm 8:1, 9).

Pause and reflect on the words of the apostle Paul to Timothy: "For there is one God, and one mediator also between God and men, the man Christ Jesus" (1 Timothy 2:5). Because Jesus Christ fulfilled the conditions that were set before Him, the Father stands pledged throughout eternity to preserve every one of those for whom His incarnate Son mediates. His standing before God is ours. His life belongs to us. He is most worthy of our praise and thanksgiving!

> *All hail to the Name Which Is Above Every Name—*
> *The Only One, forever the same.*
> *He is the One, Faithful and True,*
> *The only Mediator to see us through.*

Read the Scriptures below and write out specific ways to put the truths from today's reading into action in your own life. Refer to the *Personal Application Diary.*

[1] Zechariah 14:9; [2] Luke 12:5; [3] Philippians 2:9; [4] 1 Timothy 2:5; [5] Revelation 1:8.

Personal Application Diary

Prince of Peace
Only Begotten Son
Only God

20

The *Prince of Peace*[1] brings peace to people and nations. He is our true source of security. When we have peace with God, we need not cringe in terror nor be afraid of Him, but we must live before Him with reverence and awe. We are not at war with Him.

We can take comfort, knowing that the wicked never see peace. "But the wicked are like the tossing sea, for it cannot be quiet, and its waters toss up refuse and mud. 'There is no peace,' says my God, 'for the wicked'" (Isaiah 57:20-21). Through Jesus Christ, we have peace with God. He is to us the peace of God. There is no hope of peace apart from Him, either for individuals or for nations.

The emphasis of the New Testament is that God took the initiative to send Jesus Christ to pay the price for our sins. In doing so, He suffered in His Son's death. At the cross we see God made man in Christ. God the Father gave His *Only Begotten Son*.[2] This title is an assertion of Jesus' distinct personal deity. He is God! He is unique, the only one of His kind. We have been delivered from His divine wrath by divine self-sacrifice.

Just as the knowledge of Jesus' unique sonship controlled His life on earth as the God-Man, so also should our knowledge of our adoptive sonship control our lives today. "He predestined us to adoption as sons through Jesus Christ to Himself, according to the kind intention of His will" (Ephesians 1:5). "See how great a love the Father has bestowed upon us, that we would be called children of God; and such we are" (1 John 3:1).

The *Only God*[3] is the Creator. He is transcendent, mysterious, and inscrutable, beyond any imagination of which the human mind is capable. We bow before Him in humility, asking Him to teach us what He is like and how we should think of Him. "'For My thoughts are not your thoughts, nor are your ways My ways,' declares the LORD" (Isaiah 55:8). And again, we read, "Oh, the depth of the riches both of the wisdom and knowledge of God! How unsearchable are His judgments and unfathomable His ways!" (Romans 11:33).

> *I will be glad and exult in You; I will sing praise to Your*
> *name, O Most High* (Psalm 9:2).

God in His own person is perfect peace; He must be if He is to be the source of peace to mankind. He is grieved at the sin and corruption of the world. He is stirred to wrath at the evil of the wicked, yet He is not indifferent to the sorrows and woes of mankind brought about by evil men. Christians are not exempt from the circumstances and anguish of broken relationships. Yet, when we have a right relationship with God we can face our circumstances with the proper perspective. Circumstances need not tear us down; they can also build us up.

> *Offspring of David, the Chosen One,*
> *God's Only Begotten Son;*
> *Only God, the world to rule,*
> *Omega, the earth His footstool.*

Read the Scriptures below and write out specific ways to put the truths from today's reading into action in your own life. Refer to the *Personal Application Diary.*

[1] Isaiah 9:6; [2] John 3:16; [3] 1 Timothy 1:17.

Personal Application Diary

Power
Prophet
Prince of Life
Power of God

21

The timid Christian often fears the antagonism of others. But the reality of life on planet earth is that there is always some person, or groups of persons, whose hostile reaction the Christian feels unable to face. Whatever other powers we may meet in this life, God's power is final. He has the last word. Fear is debilitating and sooner or later can cripple the mind as well as the heart of a well-meaning Christian. Let the certainty of God's *Power*[1] make an impact on us in relation to the problems that we face at this very moment.

Israel's hope was that in the Messiah, the offices of prophet, priest, and king would be filled perfectly for the inauguration of the kingly, redemptive rule of God. The Messiah was to be both Jehovah's Anointed and the personal Deliverer. Like the prophets of old, Jesus proclaimed the Word of God. But this title connotes the *Prophet*[2] to come, who would embody both the prophetic ideal and the prophetic message. Jesus Christ clearly identifies Himself with this prophetic office in His preaching and teaching functions. He identified Himself with the rejection and sufferings of the ancient prophets of God. Not only did others recognize Him as a prophet, but He called Himself a prophet (Luke 13:33). He is indeed the prophetic Messenger of God, yet despised and rejected by men.

As the *Prince of Life*,[3] He is the author and perfecter of life. Our existence here on earth is only temporary, but we can look forward to a time when that life will be eternal. As the Prince of Life, He ushers us into a new relationship with the King who sits on His throne in heaven and on the throne of our hearts. He longs to feel our hearts throb at the thought that we are precious in His sight. May our lives be a shining testament to God's love and mercy.

The title *Power of God*[4] connotes the personification of divine strength. Creation bears witness to the great power of God over all created things. Yet, there is infinitely more power lodged in the nature of God than is expressed in all His works. May the knowledge of His power give us the confidence to make the kind of declaration Hezekiah made: "Be strong and courageous, do not fear or be dismayed because of the king of Assyria nor because of all the horde that is with him; for the one with us is greater than the one with him" (2 Chronicles 32:7).

> *Be exalted, O LORD, in Your strength; we will sing and praise Your power* (Psalm 21:13).

Knowing that God is our power, we can have renewed confidence that He is committed to deliver us from every fear. We can be assured of God's presence and power in the dark valleys of pain and trouble.

> *Prince of Peace in a world of unrest,*
> *Prince of Life, bringing man God's best;*
> *The great Prophet rejected by men,*
> *The Power of God to deliver from sin.*

Read the Scriptures below and write out specific ways to put the truths from today's reading into action in your own life. Refer to the *Personal Application Diary.*

[1] Mark 9:1; [2] John 7:40; [3] Acts 3:15; [4] 1 Corinthians 1:24.

Personal Application Diary

Portion of Jacob
Prophet of the Most High
Physician
Passover
Precious Corner Stone
Propitiation

22

The spiritual possession of the nation of Israel is the *Portion of Jacob*,[1] for from among them came the Messiah who would bring peace and reconciliation between God and man. Although Jesus came into this world in a quiet and humble way, contrary to what the Jews were looking for, He was, and still is, the Maker of all. Jesus did not lose His identity as God when He became man. He came to demonstrate His love for us and to fulfill His mission here on earth.

As the *Prophet of the Most High*,[2] Jesus demonstrates and proclaims the righteousness of God. His presence joins together the working of righteousness and grace for our salvation. The humanity of Jesus Christ sums up the perfection of the divine ideal for men.

Mankind is physically sick and in constant need of the *Physician*,[3] yet man's need for healing is even greater in the moral and spiritual realm. There, the ravages of sin are even more grim and obvious, and the tragedy of broken and painful relationships is even greater. God is the Great Healer of men. He has the remedy that can heal the body of man as well as heal his soul.

The title *Passover*[4] calls to our remembrance the events in Exodus 12, a beautiful illustration of the redemptive work which Jesus Christ accomplished at Calvary. He was God's sacrifice for our deliverance. The blood of Jesus secures for us the forgiveness of our sins and the cleansing of our hearts.

Jesus is described as the Living Stone, the Corner Stone, the rejected Stone, the stumbling Stone, and the *Precious Corner Stone*.[5] The apostle Paul uses the figure of the Church as a temple, reminding us that Christ is the corner stone, the apostles and New Testament prophets the foundation, and each Christian a living stone. In 1 Corinthians 3:11, the apostle Paul refers to Christ as the foundation.

The One who quenched God's wrath against us by obliterating our sins from His sight is the *Propitiation*.[6]

> *He has sent redemption to His people; He has ordained His covenant forever; holy and awesome is His name* (Psalm 111:9).

God's wrath is His righteous anger toward our unrighteousness. Jesus Christ shielded us from God's retributive justice by becoming our representative substitute. He paid the penalty for our sins, which was death on the cross in our stead.

Our source of power is in the risen Christ. Let us behold Him in His Word and depend on Him in prayer!

> *Prophet of the Most High*
> *Precious Corner Stone*
> *Portion of Jacob,*
> *Passover, coming back for His own.*

Read the Scriptures below and write out specific ways to put the truths from today's reading into action in your own life. Refer to the *Personal Application Diary*.

[1] Jeremiah 10:16; [2] Luke 1:76; [3] Luke 4:23; [4] 1 Corinthians 5:7; [5] 1 Peter 2:6; [6] 1 John 2:2.

Personal Application Diary

Refuge
Redeemer
Righteous Branch
Ruler
Righteous One

23

God is our *Refuge*.[1] He gives security and peace. If He were limited in strength, we might despair. But He is omnipotent. Therefore, no prayer is too difficult for Him to answer; no need is too great for Him to supply; no passion is too strong for Him to control; no pain is too deep for Him to relieve; no temptation is too powerful for Him to deliver us from.

Grace and truth were fully revealed and perfectly exemplified when the *Redeemer*[2] came to this earth and died for His people on the cross. The Redeemer brings His people back to God. In this title, we find the substance of the message of Christianity: deliverance from enslavement to sin, fear, and death.

Jeremiah predicted that Israel would return from captivity and be restored to its land and that God would raise up from David a *Righteous Branch*.[3] God's Word promises a King who reigns and brings judgment and justice on the earth. He brings peace and security to Israel and is called Jehovah our Righteousness. As the Righteous Branch of David, He identifies Himself with Israel and with us so that He truly represents us before God. In Him it can be said that we have truly met our obligation to God.

In Jesus, God promised that from Bethlehem would rise a *Ruler*[4] who would be the Shepherd of the people of Israel. God knew that we would need someone to rule over us—One who would lead us in paths of righteousness. Left to our own earthly desires, we are separated from the fold. When we allow Jesus to be the ruler of our hearts, our thoughts, and our deeds, we become witnesses of His grace.

Jesus Himself is the *Righteous One.*[5] He not only defines what is moral, He Himself is the source of morality. Righteousness is not only a part of His personal character; it is an essential element of His heavenly and earthly kingdoms. He is concerned that His people also be righteous. As *Jehovah-Tsidkenu,* He is "the LORD our righteousness." His righteousness is bestowed upon us as a free gift through our faith in Christ's atoning sacrifice at the cross. In his sermon at Pentecost, Peter accuses his hearers of denying the Holy One and the Just or Righteous One (Acts 3:14). This title reveals to us the method and the measure of our acceptance by God. We are cleansed by the blood of the Lamb and are clothed with the white robe of His righteousness.

> *We give thanks to You, O God, we give thanks, for Your name is near; men declare Your wondrous works* (Psalm 75:1).

Every Christian can say of the Lord, "For You are my rock and my fortress; for Your name's sake You will lead me and guide me" (Psalm 31:3). Yes, as Christians we have Someone whom we can rely on in every circumstance of life.

> *Righteous Branch*
> *The Righteous One for me.*
> *O Redeemer of Israel,*
> *The Refuge to whom I flee.*

Read the Scriptures below and write out specific ways to put the truths from today's reading into action in your own life. Refer to the *Personal Application Diary.*

[1] Psalm 46:1; [2] Isaiah 63:16; [3] Jeremiah 23:5; [4] Matthew 2:6; [5] Acts 7:52.

Personal Application Diary

Rock
Resurrection
Righteous Judge
Righteous
Ruler of the Kings of the Earth

24

All praise to His glorious Name, the *Rock*[1] who is forever the same. We can rest securely upon this firm and solid foundation. His purpose is fixed, His will is stable, and His Word is sure. His very character guarantees the fulfillment of His promises.

The *Resurrection*[2] is the source of new life and immortality. Because Jesus is the Resurrection and the life, His children never need to fear death or be overwhelmed by the sadness it brings. Resurrection is a person, Jesus Christ, not simply a doctrine. We can draw upon His resurrection power today. The power that raised Jesus from the dead two thousand years ago is the same power that lives in us and is available to us now.

God is the supreme ruling authority in the universe. He is both Lawgiver and Judge. As our Creator and Owner, He has the right to make laws for us and to reward us according to whether or not we keep them. God loves righteousness and hates sin. The judge who completely identifies with what is just and right is perfectly fulfilled in the *Righteous Judge,*[3] Jesus Christ.

God is *Righteous*[4] and as such He is absolutely pure and perfect. His righteousness is not fully declared until He makes His creatures righteous with His own righteousness. We cannot have peace until we first have righteousness. Because Jesus Christ died on the cross and rose again, we can have His righteousness when we place our trust in Him.

We are pilgrims on this earth waiting with expectant hearts to meet the King of glory. Let us live our lives worthy of His calling so that others may also desire to know the God whom we serve, the *Ruler of the Kings of the Earth.*[5]

> *I will give thanks to the* LORD *according to His righteousness and will sing praise to the name of the* LORD *Most High* (Psalm 7:17).

Jesus is the Rock on which we may stand when the torrents of life threaten to sweep away everything we would cling to. It would be foolish for us to put our trust in anything or in anyone but Him. Like the man who built his house on sand, when the rains came down and the winds blew, it fell with a great crash (Matthew 7:24).

> *Behold He is righteous,*
> *A Righteous Judge above man.*
> *The Resurrection and the Life—*
> *On this Rock, I will stand.*

Read the Scriptures below and write out specific ways to put the truths from today's reading into action in your own life. Refer to the *Personal Application Diary.*

[1] Isaiah 44:8; [2] John 11:25; [3] 2 Timothy 4:8; [4] 1 John 2:1; [5] Revelation 1:5.

Personal Application Diary

Spirit of God
Spirit of the Lord
Spirit
Spirit of Jesus Christ

25

𝕿he *Spirit of God*[1] is the very Person of God. The Holy Spirit was an active agent in the creation of all things. He is omnipotent. The Spirit of God brooded upon the face of the waters, and the world came into existence. The Holy Spirit is the third Person of the Trinity and this title stresses the equality of the Spirit with the Father. When He is called the "Spirit of God," this means that He is the very essence of God.

In the Old Testament, when true prophets announced divine judgment because of apostasy and idolatry, false prophets often arose and prophesied that there would be no divine judgment. In contrast to these false prophets, the true prophets of God were filled with the power of the *Spirit of the Lord*.[2] These prophets from God were filled with the Holy Spirit. They were personally involved in the life of Israel and in announcing the coming of the Lord Jesus Christ.

Since God cannot be defined in material categories, let us recognize that the *Spirit*[3] is a Person, not simply an influence or a power. We may have fellowship with Him, listen to Him, and in return love and obey Him. There is one Divine Spirit—the Holy Spirit. He is at the same time the Spirit of the Father and of the Son, since they are One. The Christian life is more than a manifestation of some impersonal power through the individual. It is the manifestation of the Person with whom the believer can have a most personal, intimate relationship. The Holy Spirit is a support to us and helps us with the battles we face in life. He is *Jehovah-Nissi*, "The Lord our banner" who provides all we need in life's daily circumstances.

All the divine truth that is in the Father is understood and made known by the Holy Spirit. He reveals what He knows concerning God.

Since He is co-equal with the Father and the Son, He is able to illuminate the truth found in the Word of God concerning both of them. All Three are One in essence and One in being. If the Spirit were merely a power coming from above, we could use it at will. But since the Spirit is a Person, and even more than that, God Himself, we can only be at His disposal. The Spirit, who is related to God, is also related to Christ, for He is the *Spirit of Jesus Christ*.[4] The Spirit possesses the same attributes that God the Father and God the Son possess. He is not less than God. There is, in the Spirit, that which is in the Father and in the Son.

> *Sing to God, sing praises to His name; lift up a song for Him who rides through the deserts, whose name is the LORD, and exult before Him* (Psalm 68:4).

God Almighty is a jealous God. He will not share His glory with anyone else. The Spirit of God shares this jealousy even as He calls attention to the Son, Jesus Christ. Let our eyes look only to His glory.

> *O Spirit,*
> *Spirit of God,*
> *Spirit of the LORD for all to see*
> *The Spirit of Jesus Christ living in me.*

Read the Scriptures below and write out specific ways to put the truths from today's reading into action in your own life. Refer to the *Personal Application Diary*.

[1] Exodus 35:31; [2] Isaiah 11:2; [3] Romans 8:26; [4] Philippians 1:19.

Personal Application Diary

Spirit of Truth
Spirit of Holiness
Spirit of Adoption
Spirit of Faith
Spirit of Grace

26

This title, *Spirit of Truth,*[1] means more than the Holy Spirit simply telling us true things. Rather, it affirms that the Holy Spirit in His being is truth. The Holy Spirit reveals divine truth to men and has come to make the Person of Jesus Christ known. As we come to know Him, we come to know the truth of God. The revelation of truth is the ministry of the Holy Spirit.

The Spirit possesses unchangeable, unalterable holiness. That quality of holiness, belonging to the Father and the Son, also belongs to the Holy Spirit. He is the *Spirit of Holiness*[2] and as such He is our Source of holy living. Are we depending on Him?

We can say with certainty that the moment anyone trusts Christ for salvation he is born again and is baptized by the Spirit into the body of Christ. The *Spirit of Adoption*[3] takes up His residence in the heart of that believer and makes him a member of God's family. When the new birth takes place, the Holy Spirit seals and thus gives hope to the believer (Ephesians 1:13-14). Among the Jews, the seal was a token of the completion of a transaction. When an agreement was completed, the seal made the contract certain. The image of the seal helps us to understand that the actual gift of the Holy Spirit is a solemn guarantee that we are God's property. We are marked off as God's possession, awaiting the day of final redemption.

God sovereignly bestows a measure of faith to each of His elect. True faith is God-directed, for it is based upon His divine grace and is communicated by the *Spirit of Faith.*[4] Biblical faith is always a response to

God's initiative in Christ. Great men and women of faith look away from themselves to the all-sufficient and powerful God.

We are called to grow and continue in grace. The Holy Spirit is a communicator of grace, and, as such, He is called the *Spirit of Grace.*[5] He is the One who quickens the elect who were once spiritually dead, opens their once-blind eyes, and softens their hardened hearts. May we rest continually in the assurance that His grace is sufficient to see us through any and all circumstances of life.

> *"A battered reed He will not break off, and a smoldering wick He will not put out, until He leads justice to victory. And in His name the Gentiles will hope"* (Matthew 12:20).

Grace is the effectual working of God's power. It is often described as being God's Riches At Christ's Expense. Grace extends favor to one who does not deserve it and can never earn it. Grace causes God's power to be perfected in our weakness. Let us praise Him right now for His goodness, mercy, and grace in our lives!

> *Spirit of Grace*
> *Spirit of Faith*
> *Spirit of Truth—only You can give;*
> *Spirit of Holiness—the power to live.*

Read the Scriptures below and write out specific ways to put the truths from today's reading into action in your own life. Refer to the *Personal Application Diary.*

[1] John 16:13; [2] Romans 1:4; [3] Romans 8:15; [4] 2 Corinthians 4:13; [5] Hebrews 10:29.

Personal Application Diary

Spirit of Knowledge
Spirit of Wisdom
Shield
Spirit of Life

27

There are no secrets that God the Father and God the Holy Spirit do not know about. There are also no secrets in our hearts or minds that are not known to the *Spirit of Knowledge*.[1] He knows every thought and intent of our hearts. What a privilege it is for us who are children of God, because His knowledge of us is not limited to the physical realm. But more importantly, He knows our inner thoughts, our desires, our fears, and our motives. When there are times that we tend to doubt our God, let us rest in the truth that the Spirit of Knowledge will give us hearts of understanding and eyes of faith to carry us through.

Everything about God is infinite, for He is the *Spirit of Wisdom*.[2] His presence fills heaven and earth. His wisdom is limitless, for He knows everything about the past, present, and future. The Scriptures are inspired by Him, and His Spirit enables us to understand them. He explains to us the things pertaining to God. He reveals to us heavenly truth that human understanding cannot fathom.

The darts of Satan are a reality, even though we may not see them coming our way, but we can place our trust in the God who is our *Shield*.[3] There is no temptation so great that He cannot shield us from it. He is our protector by day and by night. He has promised never to leave us nor forsake us.

Man is mortal, and from the moment of birth he is on his way to death, not only physically, but spiritually as well. But for the believer, physical death is a step into life. Death is a transition that leads to a fuller experience of life with God. The *Spirit of Life*[4] gives life to those who were once dead and doomed to eternal damnation. The believer possesses the same life that

God possesses. God's own existence never had a beginning, for He is the Creator. Created life had its beginning in time. Uncreated life is eternal life.

> *Therefore I will give thanks to You among the nations, O*
> *LORD, and I will sing praises to Your name* (Psalm 18:49).

The Spirit of Life possesses the same quality of life that God the Father possesses. He does not only give life—He *is* life. Since God is personal, the deepest meaning of our lives lies in His purpose for us. God's purpose for us is the final meaning for living. In Christ, we are free to live and love as we never have before. May that motivate us to tell others the good news!

> *Spirit of Life, revealing to me*
> *Spirit of Wisdom, oh let me see*
> *Spirit of Knowledge, that I may know*
> *Your Servant through whom Your grace does flow.*

Read the Scriptures below and write out specific ways to put the truths from today's reading into action in your own life. Refer to the *Personal Application Diary.*

[1,2] Isaiah 11:2; [3] Psalm 3:3; [4] Romans 8:2.

Personal Application Diary

Savior Christ Jesus
Suffering Servant
Sanctifier

28

The Gospel of salvation is very simple for those who have chosen not to depend on their good works to earn a place in heaven. Yet many of us are still lost, for we have not placed our trust in the *Savior, Christ Jesus.*[1] God calls us to repentance, for without this we will not see a need for a Savior. It is only in humble acceptance of our sinfulness that we can experience the preciousness of Christ's death on the cross.

Speaking through the prophet Isaiah, God foretold that Jesus Christ would be despised and rejected, oppressed and afflicted, led like a lamb to the slaughter, and pierced for our transgressions. He would be numbered with the transgressors and would bear our iniquities. Jesus' sacrifice on the cross was a sin-bearing death.

As the *Suffering Servant,*[2] He can identify with our feelings of rejection, persecution, or oppression, for He was also tempted and tried. Yet He was without sin. He learned obedience and was made perfect through suffering. As the Lamb, He subjected Himself willingly to the Father's will, for He was led as a lamb to the slaughter (Isaiah 53:6-7). There is no trial or suffering that we can or will go through to equal His suffering. Let the reflection of His suffering cause us to cry out with the psalmist, "For Your name's sake, O LORD, pardon my iniquity, for it is great" (Psalm 25:11).

The *Sanctifier*[3] sets us apart as children of God for participation in His character and works. God, who sanctifies His people, demands purity of life and righteousness, which becomes a reality when we yield ourselves to Him. Man's sinfulness causes us to shrink from God's holiness when we realize the impossibility of being what a holy God requires. Yet, God reassures us of His enabling power by calling us to be holy as He is holy (Leviticus 19:2).

For this reason also, God highly exalted Him, and bestowed on Him the name which is above every name, so that at the name of Jesus every knee will bow, of those who are in heaven and on earth and under the earth (Philippians 2:9-10).

Sanctification and holiness belong together because the goal of sanctification is a life of holiness. Being set apart unto God connotes the presence of righteousness that provides right thoughts, right speech, and right conduct. The Sanctifier is at work in all believers' lives, applying grace to transform them into the image of Jesus Christ. God can enable all of us to desire His will above all else, no matter how deeply embedded we may be in this world.

O Suffering Servant who died for me,
The Savior, Christ Jesus, who sets men free,
O Sanctifier of my soul,
The gift of Salvation who makes men whole.

Read the Scriptures below and write out specific ways to put the truths from today's reading into action in your own life. Refer to the *Personal Application Diary.*

[1] 2 Timothy 1:10; [2,3] Hebrews 2:10-11.

Personal Application Diary

_____
_____
_____
_____
_____
_____
_____
_____
_____
_____
_____
_____
_____
_____
_____
_____
_____
_____
_____
_____
_____
_____
_____
_____
_____
_____
_____
_____
_____
_____
_____
_____
_____
_____
_____

Stone of Israel
Shepherd
Strength
Shepherd and Guardian

29

During Old Testament times, the temple was a sacred place of worship. It was there the Jews experienced God's presence, yet in the hardness of their hearts they rejected the *Stone of Israel*,[1] the Chief Corner Stone. We too, in our own way, have hardened our hearts and rejected Him who holds the key to peace with God and with man. God in His power can change our hearts of stone into hearts of flesh that will respond in obedience to His calling.

The title *Shepherd*[2] has an enduring effect for us who have experienced His gentleness and patience in reaching out to us when we were lost. Many times, we choose to stray from the fold, thinking that we can be independent, but the Shepherd brings us back into His loving arms. The Shepherd cares for His sheep, for they are His. He knows them by name. What a joy it is to know that our God is a loving and caring Shepherd. *Jehovah-Rohi,* "The LORD my Shepherd," leads, feeds, strengthens, and comforts His flock.

To experience God's *Strength*[3] we must realize our own weakness. To experience His fullness, we must empty ourselves of any thought that would lead us to act in our own strength. This is not easy today, in a world where accepting one's weakness is a sign of defeat. But the less empty of self we are, the fewer blessings He can pour into us. The more pride and self-sufficiency we have, the less we are able to appropriate His strength. Sometimes the Lord may have to chasten us to teach us His lessons, but we can be sure that His purpose will be the most satisfying path for us to walk.

As the *Shepherd and Guardian*[4] of our souls, He meets every need of His flock, and there is no want to those who trust Him. He leads us into the green pastures of His Word and feeds us with the bread of life. He guides us into the right paths, which may sometimes be through fresh meadows, or sometimes over rough, rocky mountains and dark places. In any case, we can be assured of His continuous presence.

For You have heard my vows, O God; You have given me
the inheritance of those who fear Your name (Psalm 61:5).

We are likened to sheep, incapable of going back home without a Shepherd to lead us. What a privilege to have a loving Shepherd to guard us and guide us until He calls us to His eternal home! "For such is God, our God forever and ever; He will guide us until death" (Psalm 48:14).

Shepherd and Guardian of the sheep,
Strength when circumstances cause us to weep;
O Great Shepherd of the fold,
We find our rest in Your Stronghold.

Read the Scriptures below and write out specific ways to put the truths from today's reading into action in your own life. Refer to the *Personal Application Diary.*

[1] Genesis 49:24; [2] Psalm 23:1; [3] Psalm 59:9; [4] 1 Peter 2:25.

Personal Application Diary

Victorious Warrior
Teacher
Way
Vine
Vinedresser
Unknown God

30

The battlefield is a place where one's superiority and strength is tested. In war, one side emerges as the winner and the other as the loser. In the spiritual arena, we have a *Victorious Warrior*[1] who fights our battles, and we can claim victory in each one because Jesus won the battle on the cross. If we want to experience victory, we must first put our trust in Him. When we do, He promises to be in our midst.

We often look up to teachers, especially those who have taught us much. To be a teacher is not an easy task, especially if we want to be good role models for our students. The One who is *Teacher*[2] is the "rabbi" or the Master who not only taught truth, but lived out His life on earth in truth. As true worshipers of God, we must worship Him in spirit and in truth. We need not be left in the dark as to who God is, because He has revealed Himself to us through His Word, the Bible.

God breathed life into Adam, who started out with a clean slate. Through Adam, sin came into the world when he chose to disobey God. The natural man cannot respond to things that are spiritual, but Jesus came to solve this problem. When we place our trust in Him, we cannot go wrong, for He is the *Way*[3] to eternal life.

Jesus is the true *Vine*[4] from whom the branches derive their sustenance. The true Vine never runs dry of its life-giving nourishment. As His branches, all we need to do is to stay close to the Source of Life and to drink of His goodness and mercy. Apart from the Vine we can do nothing.

A vine's branches need to be pruned if it is to bear much fruit. Are we bearing fruit? Pruning is a process that may take time and skill and will likely bring suffering to the branches. Our Father is the *Vinedresser*[5] who encourages the vines to bear fruit. How He longs to see each branch bear good fruit—fruit that only grows as a result of abiding in Him and keeping His commandments! As we consider our own lives, let us rest in God's grace by faith for enabling us to serve Him by bearing much fruit.

God has revealed Himself through His Word and through creation. Therefore, we are without excuse. Because of our blindness and stubbornness of heart, we have chosen to worship the creature rather than the Creator (Romans 1:24). To countless people, God is still an *Unknown God*[6] who seems so far away. As believers, we are called to make Him known to all the nations so that the world can magnify and exalt His name.

> *O magnify the LORD with me, and let us exalt His name together* (Psalm 34:3).

When was the last time you talked to someone about Jesus? There is no need for anyone to go through life searching for an Unknown God, for the One True God has already revealed Himself to us through His Son, Jesus Christ.

> *All praise to the Vine bringing new life each day,*
> *Glory to the Vinedresser who tenderly lifts me*
> *along the way.*
> *The comfort of our Teacher, O how wise is He,*
> *The Victorious Warrior who makes the enemy flee.*

Read the Scriptures below and write out specific ways to put the truths from today's reading into action in your own life. Refer to the *Personal Application Diary*.

[1] Zephaniah 3:17; [2] Matthew 23:8; [3] John 14:6; [4,5] John 15:1; [6] Acts 17:23.

Personal Application Diary

Way
Wonderful Counselor
Word
Wisdom of God
Word of Life
Word of God

31

Counselors are in demand these days, perhaps because we have not learned to become listeners. People are willing to pay any amount of money to have someone listen to them. Praise God that in Jesus we have a *Wonderful Counselor* [1] who is always available to listen to our cries, to our fears, and to our doubts. He is also able to sympathize with us when we hurt and to give us sound advice and rebuke us when we need it.

The Eternal God communicates with us through His *Word*. [2] Revelation is the primary concept in this name. Jesus is the expression of God, and He is all that God is. Before man can work he must have both tools and materials. But God created the world out of nothing. A word gives expression to inner thought. A word also reveals the soul of the speaker to others. In the same way, Jesus Christ both expresses the mind of God and reveals God to man. This fully Divine Word existed from all eternity as a distinct person—Jesus Christ. He is God manifested in the flesh.

The Bible tells the story of the human race not apprehending the Light, the world not knowing Him, and the Jews rejecting Him. Yet God in His grace and mercy became man and died on the cross in order to save those who are lost, making them His children as well. He is the only *Way* [3] to God and to eternal life.

The personification of divine wisdom is the gospel, the *Wisdom of God*. [4] Man does not have the ability or foresight to anticipate everything before it happens. In addition, he does not have the power to execute his every plan. But God is both omniscient and omnipotent. There is never a need for Him to revise His decrees. He knows the beginning and the end.

Jesus is God. He is God's living message. The *Word of Life*[5] did not come into existence, He was already in existence in eternity past. He gives life because He is life.

The personification of God's message is the *Word of God:*[6] "And the Word became flesh, and dwelt among us, and we saw His glory, glory as of the only begotten from the Father, full of grace and truth" (John 1:14).

> *Some boast in chariots and some in horses, but we will boast*
> *in the name of the LORD, our God* (Psalm 20:7).

The presence of the Spirit in our lives refreshes and quenches our thirst. He causes life to appear in places of desolation. He gives nourishment to the parched and weary soul. He satisfies our souls with good things, and through all our changing circumstances, He is our dependable, unfailing friend.

> *O the Wisdom of God seen in creation,*
> *The Water of Life is He.*
> *The Way to God for every nation,*
> *The Word eternally.*

Read the Scriptures below and write out specific ways to put the truths from today's reading into action in your own life. Refer to the *Personal Application Diary.*

[1] Isaiah 9:6; [2] John 1:1; [3] John 14:6; [4] 1 Corinthians 1:24; [5] 1 John 1:1; [6] Revelation 19:13.

Personal Application Diary

_____

_____

_____

_____

_____

_____

_____

_____

_____

_____

_____

_____

_____

_____

_____

_____

_____

_____

_____

_____

_____

_____

_____

_____

_____

_____

_____

_____

_____

_____

A Personal Note

My friend, have you put your trust in Jesus Christ? Is He your Lord and Savior?

I understand that you may not consider yourself a bad person when compared with your neighbor, and you may not view yourself as a sinner. But whether we admit it or not, the Bible declares that "all have sinned and fall short of the glory of God" (Romans 3:23).

God sent His Son, Jesus Christ, to pay for our sins—yours and mine. Jesus died on the cross, but He rose from the dead and now offers eternal life to you and to me as a gift. By simply *recognizing* our need for a Divine Savior, and by *accepting* Christ's payment for our sins, the matter of our *eternal destiny* is resolved!

Perhaps you understand the facts of the Gospel, and you are beginning to see your need for a Savior. But are you willing to trust Jesus Christ alone for your salvation? The Bible makes it clear that the one requirement for salvation is faith in God's provision for you through the sacrifice of Jesus Christ.

We cannot contribute anything to our salvation. Salvation is a free gift. Yet, we must actively respond to it.

First, God calls us to repentance. The word *repent* means to change—to change your mind, to change your attitude. This involves turning from sin and turning to God by the exercise of faith. Note that when Peter preached to the crowd gathered at Solomon's temple, he said, "Therefore repent and return, so that your sins may be wiped away" (Acts 3:19).

Second, we need to believe. The word *believe* means much more than just head knowledge. It means putting your total confidence in Christ and relying upon Him alone. When Paul addressed the Philippian jailer's question about what he must do to be saved, he said, "Believe in the Lord Jesus, and you will be saved, you and your household" (Acts 16:31).

Third, we need to confess Jesus openly. When Paul wrote to the Romans about salvation, he said "that if you confess with your mouth Jesus as Lord, and believe in your heart that God raised Him from the dead, you will be saved" (Romans 10:9).

Repentance, belief, confession—together these three elements comprise what it means to believe the Gospel. Will you trust Jesus Christ as your Lord and Savior today? If you would like to do so, pray this prayer and mean it:

> *Dear God, I acknowledge that I am a sinner. I believe that Jesus died on the cross for my sins, that He rose again from the dead and is alive. I ask Jesus to take control of my life. I want this to be my "hour of decision." In the precious name of Jesus I pray. Amen.*

Personal Application Diary

Alphabetical Index

Father of lights (James 1:17) 16, 17
Father of mercies (2 Cor. 1:3) 16
Father of our Lord Jesus Christ (2 Cor. 1:3) 16
Fortress (Psalm 91:2) 68

G

Glorious (Isa. 4:2) xiii, 11, 70
God Almighty (Ezek. 10:5) 74
God and Savior, Jesus Christ (Titus 2:13) 20
God (Gen. 1:1) xii, xiii, xiv, 1, 2, 4, 5, 7, 8, 10, 11, 13, 14, 16, 17, 19, 20, 22, 23, 25, 26, 28, 29, 31, 32, 34, 35, 37, 38, 40, 41, 43, 44, 46, 47, 49, 50, 52, 53, 55, 56, 58, 59, 61, 62, 64, 65, 67, 68, 70, 71, 73, 74, 76, 77, 79, 80, 82, 83, 85, 86, 88, 89, 91, 92, 94, 95
God of Abraham (Psalm 47:9) 22, 23
God of all comfort (2 Cor. 1:3) 26
God of all the earth (Isa. 54:5) 19
God of Daniel (Dan. 6:26) 22, 23
God of gods (Dan. 2:47) 25
God of heaven (Psalm 136:26) 19, 20
God of hope (Rom. 15:13) 25, 26
God of hosts (Psalm 89:8) 19, 20
God of Isaac (Matt. 22:32) 22, 23
God of Israel (Isa. 21:10) 11, 22, 23
God of Jacob (Psalm 46:11) 22, 23
God of Jerusalem (Ezra 7:19) 22, 23
God of knowledge (1 Sam. 2:3) 25, 26
God of love (2 Cor. 13:11) 43, 44
God of our fathers (Acts 3:13) 23
God of peace (I Thess. 5:23) 25, 26
God of the Hebrews (Ex. 5:3) 22, 23
God of truth (Isa. 65:16) 25, 26
God of vengeance (Psalm 94:1) 25, 26
God of your fathers (Ex. 3:13) 22, 23
God the Father (2 Peter 1:17) xiii, 7, 8, 55, 58, 74, 79, 80
God the Father (2 Thess. 1:2) xiii, 7, 8, 55, 58, 74, 79, 80
God who is near (Jer. 23:23) 19, 20
God who sees (Gen. 16:13) 19, 20
Good shepherd (John 10:11) 25, 26
Great God (Titus 2:13) 19, 20
Great King (Psalm 48:2) 22

H

Head of the church (Eph. 5:23) 31, 32
Healer (Isa. 53:5) 28, 29, 64
Heavenly Father (Luke 11:13) 31, 32
Helper (Psalm 54:4) 14, 28, 29
High and exalted One (Isa. 57:15) 28, 29
High priest (Heb. 4:14) 31
Holy and awesome (Psalm 111:9) 65
Holy and Righteous One (Acts 3:14) 68
Holy (Luke 1:49) xii, xiv, 4, 8, 22, 28, 29, 31, 32, 47, 49, 53, 55, 65, 68, 73, 76, 77, 79, 82
Holy One of Israel (2 Kings 19:22) 28, 29
Holy One (Prov. 9:10) 28, 29, 31, 32, 68
Holy Spirit (1 Cor. 6:19) xiv, 4, 8, 31, 32, 47, 55, 73, 76, 77, 79

I

I AM (Ex. 3:14) 13, 34, 35, 95
Image of the invisible God (Col. 1:15) 34, 35
Immanuel (Isa. 7:14) 23, 34, 35
Intercessor (Heb. 7:25) 34, 35

J

Jealous God (Ex. 20:5) 37, 38, 74
Jesus Christ (Rom. 3:22) xiii, 2, 4, 5, 7, 8, 10, 11, 13, 16, 31, 34, 37, 38, 40, 43, 49, 50, 55, 56, 58, 61, 64,

Mighty God (Isa. 9:6) 52, 53
Mighty Lord (Psalm 89:8) 20
Mighty One of Israel (Isa. 1:24) 52
Mighty One (Psalm 50:1) 52, 53
Most High (Psalm 46:4) 52, 53, 59, 64,
    65, 71

ℜ

Name (3 John 7) xii, xiii, xv, 1, 2, 5, 8,
    11, 14, 16, 17, 20, 23, 26, 29, 32,
    34, 35, 38, 41, 44, 47, 50, 52, 53,
    55, 56, 59, 65, 68, 70, 71, 74, 77,
    80, 82, 83, 85, 86, 89, 91, 92, 95
Name which is above every name
    (Phil. 2:9) 55, 56, 83

℗

Offspring of David (Rev. 22:16) 59
Omega (Rev. 1:8) 2, 55, 56, 59
One God (1 Tim. 2:5) 56
One (Luke 12:5) xii, xiii, 1, 4, 7, 8, 10,
    11, 13, 16, 17, 19, 22, 25, 26, 28,
    29, 31, 32, 35, 38, 41, 47, 52, 53,
    55, 56, 58, 59, 62, 65, 67, 68, 73,
    74, 77, 85, 88, 89, 94
Only begotten Son (John 3:16) 58, 59
Only God (1 Tim. 1:17) 58, 59
Only one (Zech. 14:9) 26, 55, 56, 58

ℙ

Passover (1 Cor. 5:7) 44, 64, 65
Physician (Luke 4:23) 64, 65
Portion of Jacob (Jer. 10:16) 64, 65
Power (Mark 9:1) xiv, 1, 7, 11, 19, 29,
    32, 44, 47, 56, 61, 62, 65, 70, 73,
    74, 77, 82, 85, 91
Power of God (1 Cor. 1:24) 61, 62
Precious corner stone (1 Pet. 2:6)
    64, 65
Prince (Acts 5:31) 58, 61, 62
Prince of life (Acts 3:15) 61, 62
Prince of Peace (Isa. 9:6) 58, 62

Prophet (John 7:40) 23, 61, 62, 64,
    65, 82
Prophet of the Most High (Luke 1:76)
    64, 65
Propitiation (1 John 2:2) 64, 65

ℜ

Redeemer (Isa. 63:16) 67, 68
Redeemer of Israel (Isa. 49:7) 68
Refuge (Psalm 46:1) 49, 67, 68
Resurrection (John 11:25) 47, 70, 71
Righteous (1 John 2:1) 2, 10, 11, 17, 25,
    37, 38, 49, 65, 67, 68, 70, 71
Righteous Branch (Jer. 23:5) 67, 68
Righteous Judge (2 Tim. 4:8) 38,
    70, 71
Righteous One (Acts 7:52) 67, 68
Rock (Isa. 44:8) 13, 14, 68, 70, 71
Ruler (Matt. 2:6) 50, 52, 67, 68, 70, 71
Ruler of the kings of the earth (Rev.
    1:5) 70

ℌ

Salvation (Psalm 27:1) 4, 5, 20, 46, 64,
    76, 82, 83, 94
Sanctifier (Heb. 2:11) 82, 83
Savior (Acts 5:31) 1, 4, 5, 8, 11, 43, 82,
    83, 94, 95
Savior Christ Jesus (2 Tim. 1:10) 82
Seed (Gal. 3:16) 11
Servant (Isa. 53:11) 80, 82, 83
Shepherd (Psalm 23:1) 25, 26, 67,
    85, 86
Shield (Psalm 3:3) 79, 80
Son (Heb. 1:8) 7, 10, 11, 14, 16, 22, 23,
    31, 32, 34, 38, 43, 49, 52, 53, 55,
    56, 58, 59, 73, 74, 76, 89, 94
Son of God (Heb. 6:6) 22, 53
Son of Man (Luke 21:27) 52
Son of the Father (2 John 3) 59
Sovereign (1 Tim. 6:15) 7, 19, 22, 34,
    40, 50, 52, 53

Scripture Index

1 CORINTHIANS
1:24	(power of God)	53, 62, 89, 92
1:24	(wisdom of God)	53, 62, 89, 92
5:7	(Passover)	65
6:19	(Holy Spirit)	32
15:45-47	(the last Adam)	50
15:45	(life-giving spirit)	50

1 JOHN
1:1	(Word of Life)	92
2:1	(Advocate)	2, 47, 71
2:1	(Father)	2, 47, 71
2:1	(Jesus Christ)	2, 47, 71
2:1	(righteous)	2, 47, 71
2:2	(propitiation)	2, 65
4:8	(love)	44, 71

1 PETER
1:3	(God and Father of our Lord Jesus Christ)	17
1:19	(lamb unblemished and spotless)	16, 74
2:6	(choice stone)	65, 68
2:6	(precious corner stone)	65, 68
2:25	(Shepherd and Guardian of your souls)	86
3:18	(just)	xiv
4:14	(Spirit of glory)	32

1 SAMUEL
2:3	(God of knowledge)	26

1 THESSALONIANS
1:9	(true God)	xii
5:23	(God of peace)	26, 32

1 TIMOTHY
1:17	(immortal)	17, 41, 59
1:17	(King eternal)	17, 41, 59

Printed in the United States
By Bookmasters